THE RASTAFARI IBLE

The Books of

1) The Glory of Kings

and

2) The Utterance of JAH

Jahson Atiba Alemu I

by: Sekou Tafari

I

Library of Congress Catalog Card No.: 92-82850
ISBN - 0-94839-012-3

All Rights Reserved:
(c) 1994 - Research Associates School
Times Publications/
Frontline Dist. Intl., Inc.
751 East 75th Street
Chicago, IL 60619 USA
2nd Printing — 1996

U.K. Office and Distributors

Frontline Int'l., Inc. at Karnak House
300 Westbourne Pk. Road
London WII, IEH
England
Fax: 0712216490

U.S. Library of Congress Catalogue
in Publication Data

Alemu I, Atiba Jahson
Edited by Sekou Tafari

U.S. Library of Congress Catalogue
in Publication Data

Alemu I, Atiba Jahson
Edited by Sekou Tafari

THE RASTAFARI IBLE

The Books of : 1) The Glory of Kings
2) The Utterance of Jah

Library of Congress
Catalog Card No. 92-82850
ISBN - 0-94839-012-3

Distributed in the U.S.A.
by

Frontline DIST., INT'L, Inc.

751 East 75th Street
Chicago, IL 60619
Tel. (312) 651- 9888
Fax. (312) 651-9850

5937 W. Madison
Chicago, IL 60644
Tel. (312) 626-1203
Fax. (312) 626-1553

The
GLORY OF KINGS

A Chronology of Ethiopian Kings
From Menelik I to
His Imperial Majesty Emperor Haile Selassie I

BY JAHSON ATIBA ALEMU I
EDITED BY SEKOU TAFARI

IV

Utterance of Jah   First edition -1981

The Glory of Kings   First edition - 1985
Revised edition, 1994

Compiled as the Rastafari Ible:

The Books of

1) The Glory of Kings
2) Utterance of Jah

ISBN - 0-94839-012-3
Library of Congress Catalog Card No. 92-82850

T'dad Distributors — 'UPRISIN'
Caribbean Connection
*Shop #49 People's Mall
Fred. St. POS
Trinidad

One JAH   One AIM   One DESTINY

Published by Research Associates
School Times Publications
300 Westbourne Pk Road & 751 East 75th Street
London WII, IEH   Chicago, IL 60619

Distributed in the U.S.A. & Canada by
Frontline Dist. Int'l.
751 East 75th Street   5937 West Madison
Chicago, IL 60619   Chicago, IL 60604
Tel: (312) 651-9888 (312) 626-1203
Fax: (312) 651-9850 (312) 626-1553

V

Publisher's Note

To have the belief in a 'Black God' is to believe in oneself, to deny the existence of a 'Black God' is the commencement of denying one's true self as an AFRICAN.

For too long, we have believed in the European God, and in Michael Angelo's portrait of a pale skin Jesus. We have to begin breaking the chains of colonialism and neocolonialism by reverting to worshipping our own God/Gods, and revering our own progressive Black Kings and Emperors.

Thus, for a Rastafari to believe in His Imperial Majesty (H.I.M.) Haile Selassie I as God is indeed revolutionary and positive, and therefore totally anti-colonial in perspective.

Rastafari Live!

Sekou Tafari

for the Publisher

DEDICATION

In the name of JAH RAS TAFARI, H.I.M. HAILE
SELASSIE I, King of Kings, Lord of Lords, Conquering Lion of the Tribe of Judah, Elect of JAH
and Light of this World, I dedicate this work to the
New and Uprising Nation of RASTAFARI and to
the world for their eternal guidance and inspiration.

All thanks and praises be unto the Most High

JAH RAS TAFARI

Jahson Atiba,
Prince and Priest
of the Most High
JAH RAS TAFARI

Order of Contents

* MEDITATION *

"And I saw another mighty angel come down from heaven, clothed with a cloud and a rainbow was upon his head, and his face was as it were the sun, and his feet as pillars of fire: 2) and he had in his hand a little book open: and he set his right foot upon the sea, and his left foot upon the earth, 3) and cried with a loud voice, as when a lion roareth: and when he had cried, seven thunders uttered their voices, 4) And when the seven thunders had uttered their voices, I was about to write: and I heard a voice from heaven saying unto me, Seal up those things which the seven thunders uttered and write them not. 5) And the angel which I saw stand upon the sea, and upon the earth, lifted up his hands to heaven, 6) and swear by him that liveth for ever and ever, who created heaven and the things that are therein, and the earth, and the things that therein are, and the seas, and the things which are therein, that there should be time no longer: 7) but in the days of the voice of the seventh angel, when he shall begin to sound, the mystery of God should be finished as he hath declared to his servants the prophets."

Revelation 10:1-7

IX

INTRODUCTION

"History is the landmark by which we are directed into the true course of life."

Marcus Mosiah Garvey

"Just as a tree without roots is dead, a people without HISTORY or CULTURAL ROOTS also becomes a dead people."

Malcolm X

"EDUCATION of the YOUTH is the surest guarantee of a better life."

Selassie I

In the Spirit of Fulfillment, and through the divine guidance and inspiration of I and I Father, the Most High God, JAH RAS TAFARI HAILE, H.I.M. SELASSIE I King of Kings and Lord of Lords Conquering Lion of the Tribe of Judah, Root of David and Seed of Solomon, the Elect of God and Power of the Holy Trinity ... I Jahson forward this short chronological history of Ethiopian Kings, from Makeda, the Queen of Sheba, in the 10th Century B.C. to H.I.M. Haile Selassie I of the 20th Century A.D., as a stone in the sling-shot of Rastafari, aimed at the head of Goliath — that giant system of lies and propaganda fabricated against the African race for the past two thousand years.

X

This work is also created as a spark to ignite the fire of Truth and in the mind of the African man, that he might see himself in his truly divine and kingly nature ... and ye shall know the truth and the truth shall make you free ... for out of Zion the perfection of beauty, God has shined. The light must be shown ... the truth must be told ...

Ethiopia has been able to preserve African integrity and sovereignty as the oldest Independent Black African Kingdom and the only African Nation to have escaped the living hell of European colonization and colonialism. The Lion of Judah has prevailed ... for the Lord has chosen Zion. He has desired it for His habitation.

Thirdly, this brief chronicle of Ethiopian history is created as another stone in the pyramid of Africa's glorious history that is now being re-constructed and re-created on the sands of time, by Africans at home and abroad. Its foundation is the holy mountains of Zion, Ethiopia, where Kings reign and where the Gods so love to dwell ... Glorious things have been spoken and written of Ethiopia, the Kingdom of H.I.M. Haile Selassie I Jah Ras Tafari, and I Jahson shall mention some of them as I man write of the things which I have seen (read) touching the Kings and the King of Kings — Selassie I ... for as the light comes out of the East and shines even unto the West, so also has been the coming of the age of the Son of Man, even I and I Rastafari, Sons of the Most High JAH, through the divine mystic revelation H.I.M. Haile Selassie I, the Power and Instrument of the Holy Trinity, the King of Glory and the Lord of Hosts ... and Blessed is H.I.M. who has come in the name of the Lord JAH ... RASTAFARI SELASSIE I.

EDUCATION IS AMMUNITION

LOVE RASTAFARI AND LIVE.

H. H. JAHSON ATIBA ALEMU I

Black African Prince of Peace, Love, and Overstanding. Humble Priest of de Most High JAH, elect of God.

Book 1

THE ኢትዮ. ንጉሰ ት
GLORY OF **KINGS**

A Chronology of Ethiopian *Kings*
From Menelik I to
His Imperial Majesty Emperor Haile Selassie I

BY JAHSON ATIBA ALEMU I
EDITED BY SEKOU TAFARI

©

THE GLORY OF KINGS

10TH CENTURY B.C.:

The glorious history of the Ethiopian Empire begins with the legendary meeting of MAKEDA, the Queen of Sheba, and King SOLOMON of Israel, which meeting (also recorded in the Holy Bible, 1 Kings 10, 1-13 and 11 CHRONICLES 9, 1-12) established the ROYAL SOLOMONIC DYNASTY that has ruled Ethiopia with few interruptions until the most recent reign of Emperor Haile Selassie I (1930-1974 A.D.)

Makeda lived in the 10th Century B.C. and her story is the National Epic of Ethiopia, as related in the KEBRA NAGAST (The Glory of KINGS), an historical holy book of Ethiopia. According to the legend, Makeda heard of the wise Government of King Solomon and determined to visit him at Jerusalem "to prove him with hard questions." The result of this visit was the birth of Menelik I, who was then called BAYNA LEHKEM (son of the wise man). Makeda returned to continue her reign despite the loss of her virginity.

At the age of twenty-two (22), Menelik visited his father at Jerusalem, and was anointed and crowned KING DAVID of Ethiopia. How-

1

ever, despite efforts by King Solomon to keep Makeda's son, Menelik returned to rule Ethiopia, accompanied by the first-born sons of ALL the nobles of Israel.

The legend continues that these eldest sons of Israel brought with them the original ARK of the COVENANT, which is called "ZION, THE TABERNACLE OF THE LAW OF GOD" and which was made by Moses under divine guidance, as the material copy, in wood and gold, of the SPIRITUAL and HEAVENLY ZION, and which contains the two Tables of Law, the pot of manna, and Aaron's rod. This treasure is symbolized by a square oblong box in every Ethiopian Church.

4TH CENTURY A.D.:

Between the 10th Century B.C. and the 4th Century A.D. there was the merging of SEMITIC immigrants with the Cushite (Black African) inhabitants which produced a new culture and civilization known as the AKSUMITE Empire, and a new language called GE'EZ evolved. The Aksumite Kingdom reached its zenith in the 4th Century during the reign of King EZANA.

A panaramic view of the Holy City of Aksum

3

KING EZANA

KING EZANA was the 4th Century King of Aksum during whose reign Christianity was introduced to Ethiopia. He conquered the Nile Valley Realm of Kush (Meroe) and extended the frontiers of his Kingdom. He ascended the Throne between 320-325 A.D. and introduced the title of "KING OF KINGS".

King Ezana received a Greek and Christian education from a Syrian Christian named FRUMENTIUS, who was employed by his father, King ELLA AMEDA, and who also became co-regent. Around 333 A.D., Frumentius was allowed to go to Alexandria in Egypt to obtain a Bishop for Ethiopia. The Patriarch of Egypt, named Athanasius, consecrated Frumentius himself as the first Bishop of Ethiopia, under the name of ABBA SALAMA I (Father of Peace). First to be converted, King Ezana became Protector of the new religion.

His reign was prosperous and external trade flourished, mainly with Greek merchants. He decorated his capital with buildings, monuments and obelisks, and laid the foundations of the present cultural and religious character of Ethiopia. The GE'EZ language became vocalized and independent and among the new words introduced was "Egziabher", meaning God.

King Ezana and his brother Sayzana are canonized as saints (Abreha and Asbeha) in the Ethiopian Orthodox Church.

6TH CENTURY A.D.:

514-543: KING KALEB was the last major Aksumite King of Ethiopia, during whose reign the Empire reached the last period of its ancient glory. Language, art and architecture flourished, and Aksum then controlled traffic on the Red Sea. KING KALEB was especially known for his military expeditions into the Southern Arabia in 525 to restore Ethiopian sovereignty against Dhu Nuwas, a local prince. This victory won him fame as the defender of the Christian Faith and increased his prestige and power, becoming the third power in the Middle East after the Byzantine and Persian Empires.

Legend has it that KING KALEB abdicated the Throne, dedicated his crown to the Holy Sepulchre and entered the monastery of Abba Pantaleon, where he spent the rest of his life. He is canonized by the E.O.C. and is the FIRST Ethiopian to be recognized as a saint by the Greek and Roman Catholic Churches.

7TH CENTURY A.D.:

KING ARMAH was one of the wisest and most important rulers in the early history of Ethiopia. He lived during the period of the rise of Islam, and established friendly relations with PROPHET MUHAMMAD. His predecessor, King Ella Gabaz, had given asylum to Muslim refugees who came to Ethiopia in 615 on the advice of Muhammad; and in 622 on his ascension to the throne, King Armah agreed to Muhammad's request to allow the refugees to return to Medina. He also supported Muhammad by sending money through his ambassador. The Prophet showed his gratitude for the King's friendship by commanding his followers to leave the Abyssinians in peace, so long as they do not take the offensive. Thus was Ethiopia able to remain Christian despite the close proximity of strong Islamic States. This order was respected by Muhammad's successors and so Ethiopia was exempted from the Muslim Holy Wars.

Nevertheless, the rise of Islam and the physical isolation of Ethiopia saw the decline of the Christian Aksumite Empire, as the Arabs gained control of the Red Sea and Gulf of Aden, Ethiopia became almost cut off from the outside world, except for pilgrims travelling to Jerusalem through the Egyptian desert.

1137-1270 A.D.:   THE ZAGWE DYNASTY:

With the decline of the Aksumite Empire, a new dynasty called ZAGWE, assumed power in 1137, claiming their lineage of descent from MOSES, and established itself in the mountains of Lasta, further south, with Roha as its capital.

This period saw important religious and cultural activity, especially the excavation of the famous rock-hewn churches at Roha, which was renamed Lalibala after the Emperor who built eleven (11) such churches there.

EMPEROR LALIBALA reigned from 1182 to about 1225, taking the Throne name of GABRA MASQAL (Servant of the Cross). He later became a saint of the E.O.C.

Legend has it that Lalibala had a vision as a boy, in which he heard God's voice telling him to build at Roha rock-hewn churches more magnificent than those at Lasta and Tegre. On reaching manhood, Lalibala became a hermit in the mountains of Tegre in order to escape persecution from the reigning Emperor Harba.

In 1180 he made a pilgrimage to the Holy Land, and on his return in 1182, made a successful bid for power. The new Emperor, Lalibala, then began to put into practice his Christian ideals of voluntary poverty and charity to all men. During his reign, the main threats to Ethiopia came from the Muslim chiefs in the east and southeast and local tribes in the west. Internally, he had to deal with rebellious factions including Aksumites and Shoans. Emperor Lalibala ruled until about 1225.

The last King of this Dynasty, which ruled Ethiopia for 133 years, was EMPEROR NAAKUTO LAAB, who is said to have reigned for about forty (40) years. Legend has it that this King abdicated in favor of a Shoan prince named Yekuno Amlak.

1270-1285:   EMPEROR YEKUNO AMLAK:

This king is regarded in Ethiopian history as the restorer of the Solomonic Dynasty, being the FIRST Emperor of Ethiopia to claim descent from the Royal lineage of King Solomon of Israel and the Queen of Sheba, known in Ethiopia as Makeda. During his reign, an agreement then concluded, provided among other things for the Abuna or Head of the Ethiopian Church to be appointed by the Patriarch of Alexandria. It was not until the reign of Emperor Haile Selassie I (1930-74) that an Ethiopian rather than an Egyptian was appointed as Abuna.

His reign saw the shift of central authority from Lasta to Shoa, as the Emperor consolidated his power from the capital at Tagulat. He gave vast powers to the Church and recognized the Drum rights of the Zagwe descendants. He also had to fight off ambitious Ethiopian nobles, and the Muslims. His reign was also noted for the revival of literary activity.

1299-1314: **EMPEROR WEDEM ARAD:**
Son of Yekuno Amlak

1314-1344: **EMPEROR AMDA TSEYON:**
Son of Wedem Arad

He took the throne name of GABRA MASQAL and was famous for his heroic campaigns against the Muslims of Adal in eastern Ethiopia. He reorganized the Judicial system and encouraged literary activity.

During his reign the "KEBRA NAGAST" or "Glory of Kings", the most famous book in Ethiopia, was written by Yeshaq, the Governor of Aksum.

1344-1371: **EMPEROR NEWAYA KRESTOS:**
Son of Amda Tseyon

1380-1412: **EMPEROR DAWIT I:**
Son of Newaya Krestos

He was one of the most powerful medieval Emperors of Ethiopia. His reign coincided with the steady expansion of Christianity, as well as bitter conflicts with the Muslims of Adal, whom he fought successfully.

1412-1414:   EMPEROR TEWODROS I:

1414-1430:   EMPEROR YESEHAQ:

1434-1468:   EMPEROR ZARE'A YA'EQOB:
Fourth Son of Emperor Dawit I.

He was the greatest of the Emperors in medieval Ethiopian history. He was noted for his reorganization of the government, his literary achievements, his piety, and his social reforms. His reign saw the beginnings of the first contacts with Christian Europe, in order to counteract subversive Islamic influence.

His outstanding achievements were his religious reforms and policy. He established Church rules and regulations and also built many churches and monasteries. The great theological disputes in the Ethiopian Church began during his reign, as he encouraged interest in dogmas and creeds. He also wrote a hymn and six books. In 1450 the Emperor was anointed and publicly crowned in an ancient coronation ritual.

1468-1478: EMPEROR BA'EDA MARYAM:
Son of Zarea Yaeqob

He was famous for the many churches which he built. He inherited a stable government internally, and there was little disturbance from the surrounding Muslim States. During this period, the capital was at Dabra Berehan in northern Shoa.

1494-1508: EMPEROR NAOD:
Son of Ba'eda Maryam

1508-1540: EMPEROR LEBNA DENGEL:
Son of Naod

He succeeded his father at the age of twelve and was first called Dawit II, but was later known as WANAG SAGGAD.

Between 1520-1526, he hosted a Portuguese Mission and sought to end Ethiopia's isolation from Europe. He was more interested in cultural rather than military cooperation with Portugal, since the only Muslim resistance at Adal had been subdued after a rebellion in 1517.

In 1529, an Ethiopian Muslim named Ahmad Ibn Ibrahim, alias Gran (left-handed), embarked on a Holy War against Christian Ethiopia, capturing Harar City and refusing to pay

11

taxes to the Emperor. The Emperor's unpopularity and his military inferiority resulted in his defeat and loss of his Empire, which was then ruled and ravaged by Ahmad, until the latter's death in 1543.

The Emperor, Legna Dengel, lived in exile until his death in 1540.

1540-1559: EMPEROR GALAWDEWOS:
Son of Lebna Dengel

He succeeded his father in 1540, when the Christian Kingdom was under attack from the Muslim Sultanate of Adal. He immediately went to Shoa to raise the population against the Muslim invaders. In 1541, Portuguese assistance arrived and by 1543 Ahmad was killed and the Muslims were routed. However, Muslim and Turkish resistance continued, and in 1559, the Emperor was killed in battle.

1559-1563: EMPEROR MINAS:
Son of Lebna Dengel

He inherited the throne upon the death of his older brother, Emperor Galawdewos.

1563-1597: EMPEROR SARTSA DENGEL:
Son of Emperor Minas

He inherited the Throne at the age of thirteen (13) with the name of MALAK SAGGAD. He was a great warrior-king and devoted his energies to the safeguarding of this throne and preserving the integrity and sovereignty of the realm.

On January 23rd, 1579, at the age of 29, after some military victories, he went to the ancient capital of Aksum, and there, he was anointed and publicly crowned, following an ancient Coronation ritual, not performed since Emperor Zarea Yaeqob in 1450. Emperor Sartsa Dengel died on an expedition in 1597.

1597-1603: EMPEROR YAEQOB:
Son of Sartsa Dengel.

He was crowned as Emperor MALAK SAGGAD II on the death of his father. In 1603, he was exiled by the nobles, who disliked him for his independence.

1603-1604: EMPEROR ZA DENGEL:
Nephew of Sartsa Dengel

He succeeded Emperor Yaeqob in September 1603, but died a year later in October 1604. He had been appointed heir by Emperor Sartsa Dengel in 1597, but he was rejected by the Empress in favor of Yaeqob.

1607-1632:   EMPEROR SUSNEYOS:
Great Grandson of Emperor Lebna Dengel

After Za Dengel's death in 1604, Susneyos sought to be recognized as Emperor, but was opposed by Za Selasse and the exiled Emperor Yaeqob. In 1607 Emperor Yaeqob was killed in battle and Susneyos became the undisputed ruler of Ethiopia, with the Throne name of SELTAN SAGGAD.

He was described as handsome, well-built, intelligent and well-read; an outstanding horseman, warrior and military commander. He was a strong ruler who imposed his authority on a divided realm. His main problem was religion. He showed great sympathy for the Portuguese Roman Catholicism, which he proclaimed as the official religion of Ethiopia in 1622. He was bitterly opposed by the Ethiopian Orthodox Church, and the matter was finally resolved by the Restoration of the Faith of Alexandria in June, 1632.

The Emperor died a few months later.

1632-1667:   EMPEROR FASILIDAS I:
            Son of Susneyos.

He inherited the throne upon his father's death and worked to return the State to the Faith of Alexandria in the Ethiopian Orthodox Church. He expelled the Jesuit priests and sought closer links with the Muslim powers. Domestically, he promoted the return of all Ethiopians to the Orthodox Church and imprisoned Seela Krestos, his uncle and main opponent.

Emperor Fasilidas strongly opposed Catholicism. He moved the capital from Shoa to Gondar and reconstructed the cathedral at Aksum. Emperor Fasilidas died in 1667.

1667-1682:   EMPEROR YOHANNES I:
            Son of Fasilidas.

He succeeded his father and took the Throne name of AELAF SAGGAD. During his reign, he decreed a measure of segregation against Muslims, he obliged Europeans in Ethiopia to join the E.O.C. and continued the building of the capital at Gondar.

1682-1705: **EMPEROR IYASU I:**
Son of Yohannes I.

He succeeded his father and took the Throne name of ADYAM SAGGAD I, but was known as Iyasu, the Great. Gondar reached its pinnacle as capital city during his reign; he led many military expeditions, built churches, and sought to reconcile religious differences within the Church. He was deposed in 1705.

1705-1721: **EMPEROR TAKLA HAYMANOT:**
Son of Iyasu I.

This king, who was enthroned by the nobles in Gondar on the deposition of Emperor Iyasu I, began a turbulent period in which imperial power rapidly declined until the death of Emperor DAWIT III in 1721.

1721-1730: **EMPEROR BAKAFFA:**
Son of Iyasu I.

He was enthroned with the names ADBAR TSAGA II and MASIH TSAGA, but was better known as BAKAFFA, meaning "Inexorable." He was a shrewd ruler and he consolidated the power of the Monarchy. He was chosen by Ras Giyorgis to be his puppet king, but he outmatched him and

16

all the other nobles and reaffirmed the Imperial authority. He constructed several churches and sponsored the building of the first sailing boat in Ethiopia. The nobility hated him, but the common people and the soldiers loved him. All feared him.

Emperor Bakaffa died of ill-health in 1730.

1730-1755: EMPEROR IYASU II:
Son of Bakaffa.

He inherited the Throne at the age of seven (7) and was known as ADEYAM SAGGAD II and BEREHAN SAGGAD. During his reign, imperial power declined and his mother, QUEEN MENTEWAB, was the de facto ruler of Ethiopia. Her royal name was Berhan Mogasa, but she preferred to be called Mentewab ("Beautiful Queen").

As Queen-regent, Mentewab dominated the political scene and ruled with the assistance of her family. Their reign was characterized by relative peace and stability. The main significant event of this period was the rise and rebellion of Ras Mikael Sehul, who was defeated in 1747.

Emperor Iyasu II himself engaged in building churches and in hunting expeditions. On the death of Iyasu II in 1755, Ras Mikael Sehul became the most powerful man in the Empire.

1755-1769: EMPEROR IYOAS:
Son of Iyasu II.

On the death of Iyasu II, Queen Mentewab enthroned her grandson Iyoas and continued her rule under a new regency. Emperor Iyoas' mother was the daugher of a Wallo Galla Muslim chieftain, and his reign began a period of Galla domination of the Empire, lasting for one hundred years.

In 1767, there was a civil war and Ras Mikael Sehul gained control of the Empire. Queen Mentewab died in 1773, after powerlessly watching the disintegration of the Empire and the humiliation of her family.

King Haile Melekot (Aba Telfa)

1769-1855: ZAMANA MASAFENT:

This period is referred to by Ethiopian historians as the Zamana Masafent or "The Era of Judges" an allusion to the time recorded in the biblical Book of Judges, when "There was no King in Israel and every man did that which was right in his eyes".

The Church gave the Empire an element of religious and cultural unity, but civil wars were frequent as the feudal Lords of the various provinces reasserted their authority. Nominal allegiance was paid to an Emperor at Gondar, who was usually a puppet of one or other of the great lords.

The coming of the 19th Century saw Ethiopia a divided Empire with no central authority. The highlands, once the site of the Christian Empire, were divided into three (3) independent states:

(1) TEGRE in the north, whose best known chiefs were Ras Walda Selasse (ruled from 1780-1816), Daj Sabagadis (ruled from 1818-1831), and Daj Webe (ruled from 1831-1855).

(2) AMHARA in the north-central with its capital at Gondar. Between 1769 and 1855 the political life of this region was dominated by the Muslim Galla Dynasty from Yaju in the province of Wallo. In 1831 Ali Alula became Ras at the age of thirteen and his mother Empress Manan dominated the political scene. In 1840, she married a member of the Solomonic Dynasty, deposed the puppet Emperor Sahela Dengel, and had her husband crowned Emperor Yohannes III, and herself Empress Manan. After a few years her rule was challenged by a young governor named Kassa, who defeated her in 1847. Her son, Ras Ali, was also defeated by Kassa in 1853.

(3) SHOA in the south was ruled by WASSAN SAGGAD between 1780-1813. In 1813, SAHLA SELASSE, son of Wassan Saggad was nominated as Ras of Shoa at the age of eighteen. He assumed the title of Negus (King) in the 1830's and declared the independence of Shoa. He was fascinated by modern technology through the influence of European visitors and sought military equipment from France and England. He gave Shoa good government, peace, stability until his death in 1847 through ill-health.

Hayla Malakot, son of King Sahla Selasse, succeeded his father in 1847 and led a series of military expeditions to pacify the rebellious Galla. He assisted Ras Ali against Kassa, but fell ill and died in 1855. He was succeeded by his son MENILEK II as King of Shoa.

1855-1868:   EMPEROR TEWODROS II:
Known as Kassa before 1855.

He challenged Empress Manan and Ras Ali Alula, rulers at Gondar, and in 1847 he defeated Empress Manan and became governor of all Ethiopia west and north of Lake Tana. After five years of peace, Kassa began his struggle for supreme power in Ethiopia. In 1853 he defeated

ETHIOPIA: Principal Rivers & Towns

Ras Ali Alula and in 1855 he also defeated Daj Webe of Tegre in the north.

He successfully occupied all the provinces — Tegre, Gojam, Wallo, Shoa and Bagemder. He was crowned Emperor Tewodros II in February 1855, and not being of royal ancestry, he stressed his unique position as the "Elect of God", whom God had raised "out of the dust" to re-unify his people and save them from Muslim domination.

He was educated in the monasteries, studying the Holy Scriptures and Ethiopian history, law and traditions. He did much to justify his name "Tewodros" which, legend prophesied, was the name of the monarch who would appear to rule justly and to eradicate Islam.

He re-unified Ethiopia's Kingdom into a single Empire and was the FIRST Emperor to seek modernization through governmental, administrative and social reforms. He devoted much of his attention to reorganizing the national army, realizing that only military means could keep control of the country. He opened relations with European Christendom, but his continued detention of British prisoners, coupled with internal opposition, led to his downfall.

He was defeated by the British-Indian army led by Sir Robert Napier in 1868, and committed suicide rather than surrender. This was the

FIRST time a European country attacked Ethiopia.

Emperor Tewodros is regarded as the protagonist of modern Ethiopia.

1868-1871:   EMPEROR TAKLA GIYORGIS:
Known as Ras Gobaze before 1868.

He had rebelled against Emperor Tewodros II in 1864 and remained neutral when the British arrived. The death of Tewodros II left the Empire once more divided and Ras Gobaze proclaimed himself Emperor; with the Throne name of TAKLA GIYORGIS. He had two powerful rivals for the Imperial Throne in Menilek, King of Shoa, and Kassa of Tegre.

In 1871, he tried to subdue Tegre but was defeated by Kassa in the battle of Asem at Adwa and dethroned. He was the last monarch to reside at Gondar.

1872-1889:   EMPEROR YOHANNES IV:
Known as Kassa of Tegre before
1872.

He defeated Emperor Takla Giyorgis and ascended the Throne in January 1872 as Emperor Yohannes IV. He descended from the Tegrean royal family and was crowned in the ancient capital of Aksum. He concentrated on re-unification of the ancient empire and by 1874 he had unified Lasta, Bagemder, Semen and Gojam, demonstrating his humanity and his generosity. He successfully resisted threats to Ethiopia's sovereignty and integrity, posed by the Egyptians, the Italians, and the Mahdist Movement led by Muhammad Ahmad, the Mahdi, in the Sudan.

In 1878, Emperor Yohannes marched into Shoa, where Menilek had become King in 1865 and was claiming the title of Emperor. A compromise agreement was reached whereby Menilek submitted to him as the Emperor, and in turn he gave Menilek full independence as King of Shoa and successor to the Imperial Throne.

In 1882, Menilek and Takla Haymanot (Ras Adal) of Gojam clashed at Embabo and were rebuked by the Emperor. To check further disaffection and to strengthen allegiance, a dynastic marriage was arranged in 1882 between Yohannes' son and heir, Araya Selasse and Menilek's daughter, Zawditu.

In 1884, the rise of the Mahdist Movement saw the evacuation of British troops from the Sudan with the help of Emperor Yohannes IV.

In 1885, the General Act of Berlin began the European "scramble for Africa" in this part of the continent, and the Italians, in a move against the French, seized the port of Massawa, with British consent.

Emperor Yohannes IV died in battle, fighting against the Mahdists in 1889.

1889-1913:   EMPEROR MENILEK II:
Son of King Hayla Malakot and Grandson of King Sahla Selasse of Shoa

He was the third of the three great Emperors who rebuilt the Ethiopian Empire in the second half of the 19th Century, the other two were Emperor Tewodros (1855-68) and Emperor Yohannes IV (1872-89).

Emperor Menilek II who reigned from 1889-1913, was energetic, wise and generally progressive, which qualities gained him fame at home and abroad.

Emperor Menilek II enshrined himself forever in the hearts of Ethiopians when he defeated a vastly superior Italian army at the Battle of Adawa in 1892.

On the death of Emperor Yohannes IV, Menilek proclaimed himself King of Kings of Ethiopia and all the regional nobility swore allegiance to him except in Tegre. He was crowned Emperor on November 2nd, 1889, after which he led a military expedition and subdued the rebellious Tegrean nobles.

However, the Italians kept encroaching from this direction, having captured port Massawa on the Red Sea in 1885, and by 1890 had declared its colony of Eritrea. In 1889, Menilek sent a delegation to Europe led by Ras Makonnen (father of Emperor Haile Selassie I), seeking diplomatic recognition, but by their return, Italy had encroached the official boundary lines and claimed a Protectorate over Ethiopia in accordance with Article #34 of the General Act of Berlin, made among European States, in 1885.

In 1889 also, the Treaty of Perpetual Peace and Friendship with Italy was signed at Wechale in Wallo province. Article 17 of this Treaty became the basis of major dispute because of differences in the Amharic and Italian interpretations. Menilek refused to recognize the Italian territorial claims and denounced the Treaty of Wechale in 1893, declaring that "Ethiopia has need of no one; she stretches out her hands unto God."

The Italians resorted to the use of force and invaded Tegre in 1895. On March 1, 1896, the Italians were finally defeated at the famous battle of Adwa. Italy renounced its claim to Protectorate, while Menilek recognized the Marab and Balasa-Muna lines as the permanent boundaries of the Italian colony of Eritrea.

Emperor Menilek's victory was the most remarkable triumph by an African army over a European army since the time of Hannibal (247-182 B.C.), and brought about the downfall of the Italian Government under Crispi. In October 1896,

Empress Taitu, Menilek's Wife.

the Peace Treaty of Addis Ababa was signed by Italy, who then became the first European power to recognize the absolute independence of the Ethiopian Empire.

Menilek II extended the Empire to Sudan in the west, Kenya in the south, and the Somalilands in the east, but he was unable to obtain a port. Ethiopia remained landlocked until 1952 (during the reign of Emperor Haile Selassie I), and depended upon a railroad line for communication with the outside world, which railroad was constructed between 1894 and 1917, between Jibuti and Addis Ababa.

The last part of Menilek's reign saw the construction of buildings, a modern school, a hospital, churches, a printing press and a few industries. In 1907, he re-organized the administration of the Central Government by setting up ministries.

From 1909, during Menilek's illness, his wife Empress Taytu Betul was the de facto ruler of Ethiopia until her banishment to her husband's sick room. She gave the name of "Addis Ababa," meaning "new flower," to Menilek's new capital.

Emperor Menilek II died in 1913 of ill-health. His greatest achievement was the maintenance of Ethiopia's independence and sovereignty throughout the period of the European scramble for Africa, using considerable diplomatic skill to withstand the three neighboring colonial powers of Italy, France and Britain.

1913-1916: LEJ IYASU:
Grandson of Menilek II.

He was appointed heir by Emperor Menilek II in 1909. In 1911, when his regent, Ras Tassama, died, Lej Iyasu, whose loyalties were to Wallo rather than Shoa, assumed the role of Emperor, though still under age. He crowned his father, Ras Mikael, Negus of Wallo and alienated many Shoan nobles.

Rebellion broke out in 1916 and Lej Iyasu was deposed by the Shoan nobility, who accused him of forsaking the state religion, immorality, and the mismanagement of State affairs. In 1917 he fled and lay hidden for four years before his capture and imprisonment.

1916-1930: EMPRESS ZAWDITU:
Daughter of Emperor Menilek II.

She was the first female monarch of Ethiopia since MAKEDA, the Queen of Sheba. In September 1916, a triumvirate representing the traditional political leadership was formed and consisted of Zawditu, Ras Tafari and Habta Giyorgis, the commander-in-chief of the army. Zawditu was proclaimed Empress of Ethiopia and Ras Tafari became regent and heir to the Throne.

After the death of Habta Giyorgis in 1926, Ras Tafari became the most dominant political figure in Ethiopia, and his Coronation as Negus in 1928 and the increase of his power, reflected the realities of Ethiopia.

Zawditu became a mystic for the last two years of her reign, and died in 1930 of ill-health.

1930-1974: EMPEROR HAILE SELASSIE I:
Great Grandson of King Sahla Selasse of Shoa.

Born in 1892 as Tafari Makonnen, he was the 10th and only surviving child of Ras Makonnen of the Shoan dynasty who traced their lineage to King Solomon of Israel and Makeda, the Queen of Sheba. "Haile Selassie" was his baptismal name which later became his Throne name.

His childhood education was in the royal tradition. He learned Ge'ez, Amharic and French, and at age eight, he was ordained a deacon. He began his career in 1905 at the age of 13 when he became Dajamach (2nd highest rank after Ras) and began to show his ability and disciplined character.

In 1906, his father died suddenly and Tafari was summoned with other nobles to Menilek's court in Addis Ababa to learn more about Imperial practices. He became governor of Harar, his

birthplace, in 1910, and in 1916 was appointed regent and heir to the Throne on the deposition of Lej Iyasu.

Ras Tafari was an energetic leader and resumed the work of modernization initiated by Emperor Menilek II.

He successfully obtained Ethiopia's admission to the League of Nations in 1923, and established a printing press, a modern school and hospital, and decreed the gradual eradication of slavery.

In 1928 he was proclaimed Negus of Ethiopia and was publicly crowned.

On the death of Empress Zawditu in 1930, Ras Tafari was crowned Emperor Haile Selassie I, King of Kings and Lord of Lords, Conquering Lion of the Tribe of Judah, Root of David, Elect of God.

His Coronation was the most colorful and majestic one recorded in the history of Ethiopia, and resulted in the submission of most of the nobility to his authority.

The process of modernization continued with Ethiopia getting its FIRST written Constitution in 1931 and a new anti-slavery decree was promulgated which accelerated the pace of emancipation. This process was interrupted in 1935 when Italy, under fascist Dictator Benito Mussolini, the Duce, invaded Ethiopia and sought to bring Africa's only independent nation under Fascist domination. Facing imminent defeat, in 1936 His Majesty went, after counselling with the nobility, to the League of Nations to plead Ethiopia's cause while the army and the population continued the national resistance struggle.

On June 10, 1936, the Emperor delivered his historic and prophetic speech to the League, declaring that "God and history will remember your judgment." Indecision and ineffective sanctions by the European nations made it easier for the Italians, and His Majesty remained in exile in England, as Italy continued her forced occupation of Ethiopia.

In 1939, World War II broke out and in 1940, Italy entered the war by attacking France and Britain. Ethiopia was then granted allied status as it became necessary for Britain to defeat the Italians. The Allied Army, together with the Ethiopian Patriots defeated the Italians, and on May 5, 1941, the fifth anniversary of the Fascist occupation, the Emperor triumphantly re-entered the capital of Addis Ababa.

The Lion of Judah had prevailed once again.

After liberation and the fall of the Fascist empire, the Emperor placed emphasis on education, promising a "new era" in Ethiopian history. In 1951, the University of Addis Ababa was opened and in 1952, he succeeded in re-uniting Eritrea with Ethiopia.

In African affairs, the Emperor became known for his contribution to the cause of African Unity. He responded to the emergence of newly independent states by becoming increasingly involved in inter-African diplomacy. At the first Conference of Independent African States, held in Accra,

36

Ghana, in 1958, Ethiopia played an active role and Addis Ababa was chosen as the Headquarters of the United Nations Economic Commission for Africa.

On May 23, 1963, the Charter of African Unity was signed in Addis Ababa, also chosen as the Headquarters of the Organization of African Unity (O.A.U.), and the Emperor, who presided over this first African Summit Conference, was recognized and acknowledged as the "Father of African Unity."

During the 1960's, His Imperial Majesty made several expeditions overseas, visiting Africans scattered throughout the diaspora, including a memorable visit to the Caribbean in 1966.

Internally, however, increasing disaffection with the autocratic character of the Government, together with growing student unrest, resulted in several unsuccessful plots, and an abortive coup in 1960.

By 1974, discontent had reached new proportions, particularly among the students and the youths, and there were reports of famine in Wallo province. The mass resignation of the government was accepted by the Emperor and a commission was formed to draft a new constitution. This, however, was too late for the younger generation and the situation lent itself to a military takeover.

On September 13, after a most historic and

majestic reign of some 44 years, and at the age of 82, the Emperor was deposed and was removed to the grand palace of Menilek II by the fourth army division of the provisional military government, as it replaced his regime.

Emperor Haile Selassie I is the last monarch to sit on the Ethiopian Throne in the still unfolding legend and the glorious history of this Black African Sovereign Kingdom that has survived the last 3,000 years of human existence.

Ras Mekonen, father of Emperor Haile Selassie, led the forces in the Battle of Adawa.

2nd
DEDICATION

This work is dedicated to my two children, Jahson Berhane and Jahmoon Makeda, and to all the children of Africa — those at home and abroad — for their eternal guidance and inspiration.

JAH LIVES AND HIS WORKS MUST GO ON

Order of Contents

Book 2

The Utterance of
JAH

LORD OF LORDS • LION OF JUDAH • RASTAFARI H.I.M. HAILE SELASSIE I • KING OF KINGS •

"Give us the teachings of HIS MAJESTY, for we
no want no devil philosophy."

— Bob Marley, 1979

By JAHSON ATIBA ALEMU I
Edited By SEKOU TAFARI

"Where the word of a king is, there is power."
— Eccles. 8:4

©

ON LEADERSHIP

"The world is always well supplied with people who wish to rule and dominate others. The true leader is of a different sort. He seeks effective activity which has a truly beneficent purpose. He inspires others to follow in his wake and holding aloft the torch of wisdom, leads the way for society to realize its genuinely great aspirations."

Selassie I

"Leaders are people who raise the standards by which they judge themselves, and by which they are willing to be judged. A love of high quality, we must remember is essential in a leader."

Selassie I

ON EDUCATION

"Humanity by nature is gifted to think freely, but in order that this free thought should lead him to the goal of liberty and independence, his way of thinking must be shaped by the process of education."

Selassie I 1946

"It is understood that the independence of mind, created by education individually, will have as a result the creation of an independently minded nation."

Selassie I 1946

"Education, work and diligence are the main foundations of our national existence. We call upon all Ethiopians to send their children to the nearest school for it is suicide and a crime against the responsibility which JAH places on all parents, not to educate one's own children."

Selassie I 1946

"Loyalty inspires understanding and understanding cooperation: these are the clearest evidences of strength. But the solid basis for all lies in EDUCATION. It is education which allows people to live together, makes them avoid the pitfalls of immorality, and induces respect for the law."

Selassie I 1948

"Education of the youth is the surest guarantee of a better life."

Selassie I 1948

"No endeavor is nearer to my heart and no activity has received from me greater attention than the task of educating the Ethiopian people. Education is the mainspring of a nation's life and the guardian of its future. Education is the means whereby the potential contained in the nation's ultimate resources, its people, is realized and brought to full flower for the good of all. It demands a priority second to none and is entitled to the first command on man's energies. Without the benefits of learning, the wisdom of the past and the knowledge of the present are denied us. Without education, the freedom and equality which men seek so assiduously can be no more than half realized and the material fruits of the modern world never more than partially achieved.

The task of ensuring that all men enjoy the gifts of education is the task of us all; it knows no boundaries and transcends all barriers. Until ignorance has been eradicated, understanding and sympathy cannot truly exist among men. Without tolerance and comprehension, oppression will continue to exist, peace will not be assured. To love and to seek learning is thus to love and to seek peace."

Selassie I 1963

ON YOUTH, HEALTH AND SPORT

"Of all the good things of the world which are accomplished by the wisdom of men and which can only be realized by that wisdom, HEALTH is the divine gift which is to be found above all by those who take care to guard it well."

Selassie I 1947

"If health fails, teaching, knowledge, life itself, all come to naught."

Selassie I 1947

"The building of this stadium calls the YOUTH of Ethiopia to their sacred duty to preserve the strength of body and quickness of mind by turning away from all that weaken the body or limit the intellect."

Selassie I 1947

"SPORT being the symbol of fraternity and team work, there can be no doubt of its utility or of the sound virtues which it develops."

Selassie I 1947

"It must not be forgotten that to love sport and to safeguard the national prestige, it is indispensable to have nothing to do with alcohol and avoid all base things against which conscience speaks."

Selassie I 1947

ON THE BIBLE

"We in Ethiopia have one of the oldest versions of the Bible, but however old the version may be in whatever language it may be written, the word remains one and the same. It transcends all boundaries of empires and all conceptions of race. It is eternal."

Selassie I

"Today man sees all his hopes and aspirations crumble before him. He is perplexed and knows not whither he is drifting. But he must realize that the solution to his present difficulties and guidance for his future action is the Bible. Unless he accepts with clear conscience the Bible and its great message, he cannot hope for salvation. For myself, I glory in the Bible."

Selassie I

ON UNITY AND EQUALITY

"The best means to overcome the world's difficulties is that the world be united as in a single body. Thus, being one single organ, the nations must find the means to heal their unhappy wounds not by bits but as a whole."

Selassie I 1947

"In order to be helped one must help and in helping one is helped."

Selassie I 1947

"The goal of the equality of man which we seek, is the very antithesis of the exploitation of one people by another, of which the pages of history, in particular those written of the African and Asian continents, speak at such length."

Selassie I 1963

"Unless the smaller nations are accorded their proper voice in the settlement of the world's problems, unless the equality which Africa and Asia have struggled to attain is reflected in expanded membership in the institutions which make up the United Nations, confidence will come just that much harder. Unless the rights of the least of men are assiduously protected as those of the greatest, the seeds of confidence will fall on barren soil."

Selassie I 1963

"He who would efface the sacred work of Almighty God (JAH), he who would abuse the mysteries of JAH creation and discriminate between man and man, whom JAH created equal, on the basis of color, race or creed, calls down upon himself disaster and ruin. Let no one forget that Africans differ from no other people in the world: we love those that love us, dislike those by whom we are disliked, and we are jealous guardians of our freedom."

Selassie I

ON LAW

"The Parliament has the responsibility to legislate for the benefit and the welfare of our whole people."

Selassie I 1948

"Everyone knows that laws bring the greatest benefits to mankind and that the honor and interest of everyone depend on the wisdom of the laws, while humiliation, shame, iniquity and loss of rights arise from their absence or insufficiency ... The law, whether it rewards or punishes, must be applied to everyone without exception."

Selassie I 1931

ON THE ITALIAN INVASION

"I, Haile Selassie I, Emperor of Ethiopia, am here today to claim that justice which is due to my people, and the assistance promised to it eight months ago, when fifty nations asserted that aggression had been committed in violation of international treaties.

None other than the Emperor can address the appeal of the Ethiopian people to these fifty nations.

There is no precedent for a head of state himself speaking in this Assembly. But there is also no precedent for a people being victims of such injustice and being at present threatened by abandonment to its aggressor. Also, there has never before been an example of any government proceeding to the systematic extermination of a nation by barbarous means, in violation of the most solemn promises made to all nations of the earth that there should be no resort to a war of conquest, and that there should not be used against innocent human beings the terrible poison of harmful gases. It is to defend a people struggling for its age-old independence that the head of the Ethiopian Empire has come to Geneva to fulfil this supreme duty after having himself fought at the head of his armies."

Selassie I 1936
Address to the League of Nations

"I declare again my unshakable will; and that of my government and people to use all our efforts to put an end to the Italian adventure in Ethiopia and to restore the territorial integrity and political independence of the Empire."

Selassie I 1936

"Believing firmly that Divine judgment will ultimately reward the strong and the weak according to their deserts, I shall not give up hope of the restoration of my country's independence."

Selassie I 1937

"Those who had attacked us rejoiced in our defeat and in our tribulation. We trusted in JAH. He gave us victory. Our salvation is the Lord. Who here can fail to trust in JAH, whose judgments are all righteous and who fails not those who put their faith in HIM? Has not JAH, the mightier than the mighty, once again revealed that under the Kingdom of Heaven no one government of man is greater than another?"

Selassie I 1945

"The union of the spiritual strength of the people with the material power of the independent nation provides the firm basis for our people

51

to overcome the hardships and difficulties of life facing them in this world."

Selassie I 1948

"Ethiopia relies on Almighty JAH and Natural Justice, for upon these foundations alone can the United Nations be built and sustained for all nations both large and small."

Selassie I 1948

"Belief in the Creator is the surest foundation of any civilization. This belief preserves civilization from decay and from evil."

Selassie I 1947

ON PROGRESS

"Progress must be moral. It is important that spiritual advancement keep pace with material advancement. When this comes to be realized, man's journey towards higher and more lasting values will show more marked progress, while the evil in him recedes into the ground. Knowing that material and spiritual progress are essential to man, we must ceaselessly work for the equal attainment of both. Only then shall we be able to acquire that absolute inner calm so necessary to our well being."

Selassie I 1948

" In these modern days, there are a multitude of things published in print and broadcast by radio which captivate the human mind and spirit; many new ideas are disseminated by the learned. Many wonderful appliances are produced to make life more and more comfortable. The rich powers have passed on from exploring and exploiting this earth and are vying with each other to explore and conquer the moon and the planets. Knowledge is increasing in a bewildering manner. All this is good, wonderful and praiseworthy. But what will be the end of it all? It is Our firm belief that only what the Lord wills will be done."

Selassie I 1966

" It is Our conviction that all the activities of the children of men which are not guided by the Spirit and counsel of God will bear no lasting fruit, they will not be acceptable in the sight of the Lord and will therefore come to naught as the Tower of Babel came to naught."

Selassie I 1966

ON WAR AND PEACE

"Wars and rumors of wars are occupying the attention of governments and peoples, but the world is thirsting more than ever for peace and justice."

Selassie I 1936

"It is the will of JAH that domination by force shall perish by the same force that imposed it."

Selassie I 1936

"In very truth there are no interests nor reasons, however legitimate they may be, that can justify war."

Selassie I 1937

"In order that the work of evil may not triumph again over this redeemed humanity, all peace-loving peoples must rally together for the definite re-establishment of right and peace."

Selassie I 1937

"The world is not narrow and proscribed in nature; but man, because of self-love, has made it narrow and proscribed."

Selassie I 1948

"The universe was created for man to live in peace, concord, and happiness."

Selassie I 1947

"To win the war, to overcome the enemy upon the field, cannot alone ensure the victory in peace. The cause of war must be removed. Each Nation's rights must be secure from violation. Above all, from the human mind must be erased all thoughts of war as a solution. Then and then only will war cease."

Selassie I 1945

"Disarmament is vital today, quite simply, because of the immense destructive capacity which men now possess. Ever since the stone age, the production of arms has always been the source of man's own destruction."

Selassie I 1963

"The preservation of peace and the guaranteeing of man's basic freedoms and rights require courage and eternal vigilance: courage to speak and act — and, if necessary, to suffer and die for truth and justice; eternal vigilance that the least transgression of international morality shall not go undetected and unremedied."

Selassie I 1963

"Peace is a day to day problem, the Product of a multitude of events and judgments. Peace is not, it is becoming."

Selassie I 1963

MESSAGE TO TRINIDAD & TOBAGO (TRINITY)

Address by His Imperial Majesty Haile Selassie I, Emperor of Ethiopia to the Assembly of Parliament of Trinidad and Tobago, on Tuesday, 19th April 1966.

Distinguished Members of Parliament, it gives great pleasure to appear before this distinguished assembly and bring you the fraternal salutations of the Ethiopian people.

The peoples of Ethiopia and Trinidad and Tobago are today joined in a massive and continuous effort to create for themselves a new and better way of life. They face many of the same problems. The hopes and aspirations which they share derive from the same essential beliefs in the nature and destiny of man. It is thus inevitable, too, that there should exist between these two great peoples the strong and lasting ties of friendship and understanding. We all know, as representatives of the people, that this is a particularly critical period in the councils of the twentieth century.

The manner in which the representative of the people should properly discharge his responsibilities has long been a matter for learned discussion among philosophers and political scientists. The world of developing nations is creating new problems for the scholars to ponder as new societies are emerging on this continent today with the intricate and explosive questions of national and international development. Is the representative responsible only to the constituency or to the particular group or interest which has chosen or appointed him? Certainly in this responsibility must be an element in the thought and action of such a man that there are higher values and greater interests and responsibilities than these.

Sectional and divisive factors often cause major obstacles to national development in their expanded sense, as narrow national and ideological interest may threaten even, national unity and progress.

No one today is so foolish to believe that any one nation constitutes a perfect monolith of faith and ideology nor could anyone wish that there should be such utter unity of thought and aspiration. The systems of Government which have sought to impose uniformity of belief have survived briefly and then expired, blinded and weakened by excessive reliance upon their supposed infallibility. The only system of Government which can survive is one which is prepared to tolerate dissent and criticism, and which accepts these as useful and in any case inevitable aspects of all social and political relations. The tolerance of dissent and criticism within a Government proceeds from a singular social phase — that the Government exists to serve the people generally.

Government servants whether designated as representatives or not, have the trust to work for the general welfare. The same trust exists among the member states of international organisations and the national community. The members of such organisations must adhere to some tacit or expressed conception of international welfare. In the case of the Organization of African Unity it is the national welfare. In the case of the UN Organization it is the world welfare. In one way or another the member nations must accept in thought, in spirit and action the basic premise of their institution. Namely that men of all races, beliefs and status share some essential goals in common.

From this premise no great or easy actions follow as corollaries. The representatives of people and nations can only come together with open and objective minds and willing hearts to engage in dialogue without rigid dogmas and slogans and without violence. Working this way achieves no instant utopia. It may, however, enable us to achieve together what it is possible to achieve, and to move forward steadily if not always in great haste, with some degree of harmony and mutual understanding. Domestically, we can build strong and happy and resourceful societies. Internationally, we can force the end of oppression of man by man and nation by nation. We can bring about the peace, security and mutual trust which will open the way to the greater human achievement for which the needs of mankind now cry out.

Distinguished Members of Parliament, permit me to take this opportunity to express my heartfelt gratitude for the reception that was accorded to me by the people of Trinidad and by the Government-and Tobago, which we are going to include in our visit - I hope this will serve as an example for strengthening relations among nations that are dedicated to the same essential voice. Thank you.

Selassie I
1966

ON AFRICAN UNITY

"Unity is the accepted goal."
Selassie I (OAU)

"Today, we look to the future calmly, confidently and courageously. We look to the vision of an Africa not merely free but united. In facing this new challenge, we can take comfort and encouragement from the lessons of the past. We know that there are differences among us. Africans enjoy different cultures, distinctive values, special attributes. But we also know that unity can be and has been attained among men of the most disparate origins, that differences of race, of religion, of culture, of tradition, are no insuperable obstacles to the coming together of peoples. History teaches us that Unity is strength, and cautions us to submerge and overcome our differences in the quest for common goals; to strive with all our combined strength for the path of true African brotherhood and unity."
Selassie I (OAU)
1963

"Memories of past injustice should not divert us from the more pressing business at hand. We must live in peace with our former colonisers, shunning recrimination and bitterness and for-

60

swearing the luxury of vengeance and retaliation, lest the acid of hatred erode our souls and poison our hearts."

Selassie I (OAU)
1963

"Let us not deny our ideals nor sacrifice our right to stand as the champion of the poor, the ignorant and the oppressed everywhere."

Selassie I (OAU)
1963

"Principles alone can endow our ideals with force and meaning. Let us be true to what we believe, that our beliefs may serve and honor us."

Selassie I (OAU)
1963

"We remain persuaded that in our efforts to scatter the clouds which dim the horizon of our future, success must come, if only because failure is unthinkable. Patience and grim determination are required and faith in the guidance of Almighty JAH."

Selassie I (OAU)
1963

ON RACIAL DISCRIMINATION

"Until the philosophy which holds one race superior and another inferior is finally and permanently discredited and abandoned; until there are no longer first and second class citizens of any nation; until the color of a man's skin is of no more significance than the color of his eyes; until the basic human rights are equally guaranteed to all without regard to race; until that day, the dream of everlasting peace and world citizenship and the rule of International Morality will remain a fleeting illusion to be pursued, but never attained; until the ignoble and unhappy regimes that hold our brothers in Angola (now liberated), in Mozambique (now liberated) and in South Africa, in subhuman bondage, have been toppled and destroyed; until bigotry and prejudice and malicious and inhuman self-interest have been replaced by understanding and tolerance and goodwill; until all Africans stand and speak as free human beings, equal in the eyes of all men, as they are in Heaven; until that day, the African continent shall not know peace.

We Africans will fight, if necessary, and we know that we shall win, as we are confident in the victory of good over evil. "

Selassie I 1964

THE ULTIMATE CHALLENGE

When I spoke at Geneva in 1936, there was no precedent for a Head of State addressing the League of Nations. I am neither the first nor shall I be the last head of state to address the United Nations, but **only I have addressed both the League and this Organization in this capacity.** The problems which confront us today are equally unprecedented. They have no counterparts in human experience. Men search the pages of history for solutions, for precedents, but there are none.

This, then, is the ultimate challenge. Where are we to look for our survival, for the answers to questions which have never before been posed? We must look first to Almighty God, Who has raised man above the animals and endowed him with intelligence and reason. We must put our faith in Him, that He will not desert us or permit us to destroy humanity which He created in His image. And we must look into ourselves, into the depths of our souls. We must become something we have never been and for which our education and experience and environment have ill prepared us. We must become bigger than we have ever been: more courageous, greater in spirit, larger in outlook. We must become members of a new race, overcoming petty prejudice, owing our ultimate allegiance not to nations but to our fellow men within the human community.

Selassie I 1963

63

EPILOGUE

Since 1974 His Imperial Majesty Haile Selassie I has taken His most rightful and exalted place as the Most High God-Head for all Ethiopians (Black People) both at home and abroad, even I and I Rastafari, who acknowledge H.I.M. as the King of Kings and the Lord of Lords, the Conquering Lion of Judah, the Root of David and Seed of Solomon, the Elect of God and the Universal Defender of all the downtrodden and down-pressed people of the Earth.

His name, JAH RAS TAFARI SELASSIE I, is become the Word of God and the rallying cry of all who stand for Universal Equal Rights, Truth and Justice.

Through the Power of His Holy Spirit, His Imperial Majesty Haile Selassie I continues to reign on Earth as in Zion, in the manifestation of I and I Rastafari, a scattered people called by His name and chosen by HIM for the regeneration of righteousness in the Earth.

By this wonderful and marvelous work, His Imperial Majesty reaffirms His Divinity, ensures His immortality and so, fulfills Prophecy.

The Lion of Judah has prevailed in this time, and forever shall be SELASSIE I JAH RAS TAFARI, everliving, everfaithful and eversure.

64